# METROPANTHEON

# METROPANTHEON

## STEVEN ARTELLE

Clarise Foster, Editor

*Signature*
EDITIONS

Cover design by Doowah Design.
Photo of Steven Artelle by Alea Cardarelli.

Acknowledgements
Some of these poems were first published in *Acta Victoriana, Bywords, Contemporary Verse 2, filling Station, FreeFall, Literary Review of Canada, Ottawa Arts Review, ottawater, Peter F. Yacht Club, The Reas'ning Engine* (Technoccult), and *Vallum*. The "Chinatown Zodiac" series was exhibited at the Daily Grind, Ottawa, as part of the 2013 Chinatown Remixed Festival. My thanks to Jennifer Stone and Drew Mosely for contributing to those poems. My thanks as well to Clarise Foster and Karen Haughian at Signature Editions, and to Rhonda Douglas for helping to turn this book into a book. Thanks, Vivian Vavassis, for the creative exchange that fuelled many of these poems, and to all the folks in Ottawa's literary community for inspiration and support. Thanks most of all to Melanie Brown—I wouldn't have written this collection without your insights, your encouragement, and your ass-kicking.

This book was printed on Ancient Forest Friendly paper.
Printed and bound in Canada by Hignell Book Printing Inc.

We acknowledge the support of The Canada Council for the Arts and the Manitoba Arts Council for our publishing program.

Library and Archives Canada Cataloguing in Publication

Artelle, Steven, author
         Metropantheon / Steven Artelle.

Poems.
ISBN 978-1-927426-40-1  (pbk.)

      I. Title.

PS8601.R835M48 2014     C811'.6     C2014-900948-8

Signature Editions
P.O. Box 206, RPO Corydon, Winnipeg, Manitoba, R3M 3S7
www.signature-editions.com

# Contents

## when graffitichild led them out on the girders

## Chinatown Zodiac

# if graffitichild didn't engineer monsters

when graffitichild led them
out on the girders

# metropantheon

the universe is a leather rabbit
with no safety measure
just the road salt stars
       blackwintered
to keep all the other gods hostage
a distance calculated in degrees
of absolute heartbreak

it can only get so cold
before love arrives with every muscle
even for the rabbit
       kindledivinity
in the lonely dark
whistling so impossibly high
only liars hear it

the stray dog still happened
scavenging the alleys of the sky
until she sounded that rabbit with bones and ears
       heartjawed
and bounded and folded him into her mouth
everywhere her affection pierced
a perfect design of teeth fitted in flesh

uncoiled all the sire rabbit's prolific seams
heights and arteries and hurtling vertigo
every incision a city
       metropantheon
their jugular graffiti of gods written into circulation
leather skinned children of the wounded rabbit
in the infinite mouth of the raptured dog

# civilization

civilization was just scaffolding
when graffitichild led them out on the girders
herself expressed himself
with one hand the aerosol angelic
himself impressed herself
with one hand the wet cement of the world
and with his first her first alphabet
to the androdgynation entire
declared the summer of civilization

creation you could hear it everywhere
infinite three-chord pop song infinite
and every hand with skin synchronized
clapping the intro of everything
onetwo one onetwo one onetwo one
sacred that blueprint summer
graffitichild taught them all to dance
in their rollerskates and hooves
inspiration incorporated

and taught the code of roadwork sublime
she said he every painted chevron and broken line
is the sign of our presence
metroprolific congestion and grace
abundant even to the cracks of the sidewalks yet to come
sang pick something you're good at
and make them remember your name
and demanded graffitichild divine
someone get the lights

# heavenmonger

so a demon threw the switches
with a good arm too and beautiful
levering the alloy of light and dark
into the crucible of the first city

and forever the molten sun
cast into bars of light
and forever the shapes of the moon
machined in the dark

for radiance and strength
steadfast demon of I-beams
for resolution I pray to you
forged as I am from your skyiron

# storytraveller
## for C

nomads who lose their way
or who linger against the uprooted season
travel from fact into legend
an inconceivable distance in the mouths
of thirsty witnesses
exotic among the exotic

imagine her impossible identity
a shibboleth whispered in history's deaf ear
under flamenco chords of sunlight
her presence like a shelter of silk
unraveling slowly over the warm desert wind

no legend without a city
no city without a market
no market without an oracle
she arrives with mediterranean eyes
and perceives the astrology of jupiter figs
apples of saturn
mercury olives
pomegranate mars
blackberry venus
and speaks the dialect of salt
to the leather masons
to the spice architects
to the paper jugglers
and appreciates the butcher's pottery
weaves the smell of bread into her hair
eases the crest of her wrist into the fisher's basket
and wades up to her thighs in bolts of cloth and milk
toward the carnation breeder
among the horns of perfume
and the cages of wine

all this in the midnight accounts of merchants
who watch her with closed eyes
long after their books are shut
on the day's abundant traffic

that hour of clay
when an impression on the distant sky
is a passage recorded in her script
an oasis of immortality
distorted by ruined troubadours
illegible to diligent scribes
forever the storied sanctuary of the lost nomad

# stepping on cracks

it is the nature of cities to be inhabited
configured in the lines and cracks
of every sidewalk
are backbreaking angels

transfixed to teach mothers and fathers
to streetproof their lineage
on pain of paralysis
a generation of godfearing pedestrians

# mosquito drift

cars clicking slow as prayer beads
along the unravelling boulevard
index of gravel below
thumb of gathering thunder above

slow as death with her stripper eyes
the traffic hesitates on the hips and shoulders
of humid detour lanes all summer
the skin intersection of dust and oil

and I swing at the sexless curve
of mosquitoes drifting slow as dandelion seeds
or the smell of lilac bushes sweating
impossible to brush from the air

across our city I dream an arc
this daily commute of passion and prayer
insatiable as dogs and rabbits
knowing the slow sidewalks will be revised

# the evidence of windows

hinton north and wellington where I hoped to make you the
    subject of new bricks in an old wall
it was the burg and so it was july birdcircles and the onestory
    street of dogwalkers

and it was the summer no one was anywhere and it was waiting
there were no commitments from one restaurant to the next so
    it was bikes and uncertain traffic

and ornamental families and the oldschool and past the patios
    the noble stagger of addicts
and even the heat finished early as all the gallery blinds came down
    on the hydrant shadows

and the ceiling of the sky retreated from every bylaw and it was
    the light on the last of the market flowers
and the takehome place and the maybe house had bright redbricks
    where windows used to be

and it was your name over and over that afternoon and so it was
    maybe you as I eavesdropped and maybe missed my calling
until the part about how we make the wrong decisions and
    live with it or not in the acoustic dark and the part about love

and even so it was a drop into beautiful nightchurch and the taxi
    under the dragonarch
and the backseat crosshatch tides of shadow and somewhere
    yes you with all your skill have every window bricked up

and even so the sunmoon in the broken mortar of the clouds and
    the leftover stars and the cornerstore
it was the lost view at hinton north and wellington and it was
    about you and me unable to lean out

# Free Hotel

the angels of surgery stitch windows
in the arson yellow heights, their needles
radio bright where the gears of the wind
are stripped, while above the frequency shines
an incision they've christened Free Hotel

its frame is pierced with miracles: the road
glows beneath the fingernails of lost souls
discovered in the porcelain scatter
where deliverance teems, revolving through
its siren gestures for the multitudes

the tower operates with a razor's
influence: behold the fatal impulse
severed while the keen of the defeated
is cured: even kamikazes renege
for all their wounds close up in Free Hotel

# heat

a city constructed with slabs of fat
the whole thing slathered together
and wobbling under the eyeless mortar of the sun
greasy bright as fellatioed fingers
and the juice spilling from anything that moves
because the temperature is a steak knife
all our enslaved meat shoulders through
the avatar of city heat as oppressed flesh

and he's up there somewhere
in the agoraphobic vacuum
occupying the upper stories
as though the windows are painted shut
the avatar of city heat as an invalid
sundowning in the tarantula light
of pillared newspaper and a sect of cats
until the air itself is heresy

or that indolence at large
on the wavering margins of landfill grass
a full furnace demigod
the avatar of city heat as a poet
reclining out there in the distorted wildflowers
with the insect hum of a hydro tower in his teeth
or staggering in the pseudo-wilderness
where ditches overflow with songs of septic frogs

and all summer the mosquito parliament
gladhands in gothic backyards
as the barbeque circuit negotiates its infidelities
with citronella smiles and bags of blood
and beds exchanged for smog and the sun's paranoia
the avatar of city heat as an adversary
shining the golden light of a hidden agenda
through every angle of his sweaty lens

or out on the infatuated concrete
stealing everyone else's fire
the avatar of city heat as a young executive
checking the voltage of his black plastic profile
endlessly in the reflective media
and still unfulfilled and arrogant as dry lightning
aware there's nothing any of us can do
to avert his conditionless backstabbing

every night you tie us to the searing train tracks
with fingers dark as braided fire
and unfold your kerosene instruments
and twist your thunderhead moustache
as though to swallow us with your extra tongues
the avatar of city heat as a ripper
his synchronized coal smoke on the smothered horizon
one more heroless night

# wildfires

### i

secretly monday morning
somewhere something is on fire

maybe a wooden angel
with dry venetian blind wings

became tangled overnight
in this picket fence city

when the matchstick dawn was struck
all through the splintered skyline

### ii

maybe the nevermore man
the vagrant arsonist-king

with skingraft smiles billowing
inside his coat of ashes

clutched to his ember entrails
a contraband inferno

aerosol can and zippo
emblazon every alley

iii

maybe domestic hazards
kindled this conspiracy

somewhere behind the drywall
wires spray fireworks like spores

smells like a manifesto
today is the regime change

the sirens did not receive
the propane communiqué


iv

with my scorched earth policy
maybe I am those wildfires

could explain my cinder wings
the glowing seams of my coat

my inflammable brown eyes
filled with charred propaganda

staring up at sunset birds
aimless as flaming arrows

# the arson treatise

### i

Because of dreams of a twilight desiccated by ozone and a blowtorch wind. Dreams are more flammable than anything. There's my grandmother, fuming as if the lightning were coming for her. I'm impressed.

### ii

Because sleep is punctured like a can of paint thinner. I sleep in a bed of battery acid. I rattle all night like a ball bearing. The house is afraid of the amber smell of my fingers, so I keep them close to my face. I'm inbred. I'm an outline. I'm a stop sign on Duke Street some nights.

### iii

Because of the lure of sirens orphaned across backyards for crumbled briquette faces on a forgotten porch. Weeks of the same. Before you see God you'll hear the Banshee. Salvation eats mourners whole.

### iv

Because smoke heels like an old campfire dog and licks my starving eyes. A black Labrador chased me and the newspapers scurried. Inhale all the ink you can. Impress your friends. Defy the babysitter with button eyes and a snowy television arrogance. Peel the age from your cheeks.

### v

Because my version of the landscape is runny. Lists are hazardous. A propane silhouette, a sore throat, a bank of spinning lights, a phone booth, a hero's welcome.

## vi

Because creation is a chimney stuffed with furniture. The wild, wild, wild, wild planet is the first to go. Only Skipper the dog watched and waited, though even he falls to his death and disintegrates. Autumn's amnesia does the rest.

## vii

Because the sky is a magnifying glass aimed at my back, sifting me into the sidewalk like a carbon leper. With their gift for language the shape has been christened by the Japanese. Something I can't pronounce.

## viii

Because there are never enough parking lots and hardly enough ghosts. Things haunt me, like brief messages of goodwill. Hope you are well and that this card helps bring you some comfort. We are thinking of you. We'll send lightbulbs. A trick like a brittle-skinned eyesore. Make copies. Make copies. Make copies.

## ix

Because a phoenix is only as impressive as the first match. This is a dumping ground. A septic uprising. Worse than too great a quantity of seed. Worse than a snake in the belly, or living until the next Sunday.

## x

Because I talk to God the old-fashioned way: in pillars of smoke. God is an arc welder. He's the long bus ride. He's the tinted ceiling riding you riding me. Lean from seeing others eat, I adhere to skin like a terror from beneath the earth.

## xi

Because anything that isn't kindling is a trophy. The sweetest corrosion is a bruise that won't heal, the penny caught in your throat, a night inhaled like a lung full of Scotch. Where lockjaw loosens the highway's tongue, that's where yellow and yellow and yellow returns like the same alcohol sunrise.

## xii

Because of the colour red. This smile of mine is a violent gestation, full of someone else's teeth. Half the things I have in store for you I have stored. The other half will be performed by someone else. One hundred and seventy years and a postcard. On a good day.

## xiii

Because sometimes the lights were enough. Because everything burns. Nothing else.

# long-lost infected princess

meanwhile the goddess of love
in the cold with catscratch legs and red lace
withholds the tetanus shot I prayed for
the whole audible night

until cans roll like broken bells in the gutter
and she is gone her vagrant way
staggering in the skunk sunrise
the rusting witch with her garbage day incense

pulling staples from telephone poles
with naked teeth and red fingernails
desperate to kiss everything goodbye
knowing we will all be in love at the end of the world

# nature is rusting

this autumn oxide
crumbles like a fender

the mechanic wind
hammers sparks
from iron limbs

only the roof will be preserved

# air rights
## (the cult of rabbits versus the cult of dogs)

jets heard and seen are jets
but heard and unseen
means something else
commutes the jetless sky
that slow drumroll
is the engine heart
of the archangel of skyscrapers
who tunes the wires
that stretch every tower
from every rooftop secured
straight up to every hooked star
and the moon between the cables
on the billowing ledge of night
shuffles sideways like a jumper
to avoid her scissorblade wings

angels heard and seen are angels
but heard and unseen
means something else
motivates the angelless sky
according to the cult of rabbits
paradise is under construction
while to the cult of dogs
god is protecting the yard
for whoever owns the soil
it is theirs up to heaven
and down to hell
amen says the whole credulous city
and me without a heresy to believe in
always hearing and seeing
jets everywhere

# one day the ghost of vandalism will be avenged

did you wait for me there in the lamia city
resisting the downsized tide, the sluggish Queensway drive
emptying into neighbourhoods where streets stabilize
regular as the receding Ms of preschool geese

back as far as that apprenticeship of clay highways
your fingernails scoring cities on the roof of hell
moth graveyards and long afternoons of infrastructure
ingrained much deeper than those infinite sandbox roads

transferred to well-versed transit passenger, credentials
forged like the tragic hole you shave in the frosted glass
every night the river offers you its ancient curve
that jagged promise, quiet as a drowned cathedral

if God had you beatified electronically
patron saint of static or some other grand design
would my anxious prayers find you in every direction
bending dense bus mall crowds around your relentless pose

your position in this city so hard to define
the uncivilized civil servant divinity
brilliant as a river of kerosene on Sparks Street
dark as a whitewashed alias on a Byward wall

the scar of speech healed against the bricks, still legible
in the stream of wounded copper, that lamia shape
haunting as the sandblasted sun, made hoarse with screaming
one day the ghost of vandalism will be avenged

# last december
### for John Newlove

the trunk that holds you
that grey december bark
lowers its shadow over
every cut down street
this one above all has fallen
like a beam swung down against
a december storehouse door
leaving an arc of cloud an inch deeper
in this year's wooden sky

now that your december is endless
the intemperate wind renounces the season
and peels the city like fruit
its wet fingers up under the roofs of Somerset
spraying birds against the splinters of rain
as if to show that all harvests fail
everything is more ripe in decay
whole banquets fall off the wagon
and wonders cling like seeds even to grief

how else did that black dog arrive
to stretch its grim leash across my path
animus of obscure routes
and the only light on this lumbering avenue
is the psychic's neon sign
these promises stacked like cordwood
what else but the wind waking us all
before next year's chainsaw milk teeth
freeze everything into paper

# Ganesha City

I begin with a catalogue of faults
      for this skyline of broken tusks

for the ice under the heavy roads creasing its way to the air
      serene as ruined eyes

for the sidewalks studying the way trees age the daylight
      this shattered script of elephant skin

for the radiant arms in the drywall
      an apparition's journey through the plaster avenues

for the same mistakes trafficked year after year
      in the crosshatched comfort of routine

I am the snow that falls on the ground
      yielding to every wayward track

you are the snow that falls in the branches
      revealing with gentle force the cracked beauty of the world

# muse in steam

march remembers nothing of its history but winter
in this city of salt ghosts and crying cement
amnesia is the season before summer
cold like walking through plate glass
a marathon of finish lines shattering step after step

the muse in steam remembers for me
in her bluegold sheet of burning water
skyclad portrait in porcelain frame
the furnace of glass stirred by my hand
until her eyes open and the skin of everything whispers

# wherevering

nostalgia's clenched fist in the rain this year
       wherevering
       in the skyblind up there ideal
until even longing almost is hoarded dry

except you and the sudden river of your back
       wherevering
       in the rapids of unpredictable clothes
flashflood in the mouth of this thirsty city

soon rescue's unconditional condition
       wherevering
       in the great reserves of almost rain
until even our bare hands are catching fire

# St. Patrick king of kindling

the fire before St. Patrick's Day
just over the St. Patrick bridge
just before the supermoon

it just keeps getting worse
the cat and dubious art are safe
everything else is at speed in smoke

cans of paint in a neighbour's lungs
students blinking pocketwatch tears
a wedding dress haze through a bus window

this supernatural communication
up the fallen length of the avenue
the distance between things defied in the clouds

or measured in units of safety
on one side the police hold the toxins in with yellow tape
on the other pedestrians are free to inhale

even history is billowing toward its place in the sky
toward the king of kindling
St. Patrick's invisible vicinity

no blasphemy
just expropriation by fire
that's what cities do

St. Patrick developer
with your billowing torch
of pathological urban planning

you leave us bread and roses
and maybe the barber shop
pending the marshall's augury

the sifting of barbeques reduced to charcoal
the black crush of the jewelry repair
veined with diamonds to be mined a second time

St. Patrick scatterer of bricks
with our accidental faith
we'd reclaim every burnt offering if we could

but we can't predict these things
look how fast the spring clouds are leaving today
like they know something

# you could have been a poem about Montreal Road

happy anniversary you hunter-gatherers
or whatever subsistence festival we have here
between the Rainbow Street dead end and North River Road
roughly, our stretch of name-calling and finders-keepers

you could have been a poem about Montreal Road
but now you hollow men's eyes like an apparition
in stories about a friend of a friend of a friend
and a hitchhiker who disappears at the doorstep

it's what we did to our hearts in the nineteen nineties
casually, that left nothing but forms to fill out
so dance like you're Victorian pugilists, you saints
of the staggerer kingdom, you songless walkingjays

even the woman crouched under the fire mural
is someone's the-one-who-got-away, same as you're mine
you were caught in the machinery of government
and I was up every night inhaling heart attacks

now outside the two hundred and twenty volt depot
cursing the death of culture with franglais precision
I'm talking to myself and not talking to myself
(motel, motel, intersection, necklace of fistfights)

it's always only you I'm talking to, my fourth wall
the shattering girl, posed in your still life with panic
while developers gentrify all your addictions
and I proclaim forever our chain reaction day

till then I'm up every night with the hitchhiker's ghost
writing a history of angry men: doorkickers
whitehats, overseers, the taxistanding blackhearts
prescriptionauts, blindflyers, and young explosioneers

creole Jesus of the bingo and the blue door church
give us rings for pawn shop coins, pawn shop coins for all-night
coin wash cycles, coin wash cycles for clean clothes to pawn
at the ten-dollar-fashion, ten dollars for a ring

tell the legend of salarymen who make it home
in time for dinner, their hands smelling like their own hands
and if there's a god he's the all-day-bacon-and-eggs
who sends us a straight-down rain without a lie on it

my one regret is how long I regretted nothing
so let the traffic calming parade begin at last
and I'll love you with the landlord's invasive neglect
though you change your name wherever you can catch a ride

# demolition

what is there like us in this whole city
what else is there that lays the foundations in the fall
and mines them as soon as spring arrives
it's not that we adhere to a ritual
it's the ritual that adheres to us
we must be the gods of something

# Chinatown Zodiac

# cornerstone rat

in origin stories they say this neighbourhood was vertical
somewhere around Preston
everything was tilted straight up to heaven
and the only animal in the world
was the cornerstone rat

everything after that
I can't remember

the part about how things settled down

> how old was I
> when you asked me to hold that ladder
> that's a lot of responsibility for a kid

that's the beginning of things

# oxopolis

an age of handstands
and spontaneous cartwheels
when the ox that plows the avenues
unfolded the breathing clay
making a straight line called Rochester Street

how he dedicated his foaming shoulder blades
and the vast degrees of his directional horns
scoring the urban earth
while we celebrated
the first harvest of bricks

singing: if streets are going to mean anything
let them know we were there when it happened

# tiger hypothetical

if we sit here any longer, someone will fill the windshield with tea sets
    (or fading layers of convenience store advertising)
the mural on the corner is moving faster than we are
    (right away there are things I like about you)
our conversation about the natural predators of everything we build
    (ice eats road, rust eats car, fire eats everything)
your carnivorous laugh and death-defying lines of reasoning
    (time has the biggest teeth, traffic eats time)
consolation in the grip of rush hour on Booth Street
    (everyone but you despises a commute)
creeping along until the instinctive leap through the lights at Eccles
    (because: red means stop, green means go, yellow means tiger)

# supernatural rabbit

the broth shook in every pho bowl
     in the halo of Upper Lorne

wax boxes outside the market
     fell like fans of white mahjong tiles

the roastery windows shuddered
     and the wall of theology cracked everywhere

as though to release paper fortunes from the mortar
     that summer day a supernatural rabbit fell

from a rabbitless summer sky
     and cried: a moment ago it was heaven everywhere

we were a halo of rabbit dancers in our hundreds
     now tell me what place this is

# curatorial insomnia and the dragonesque

zero stamina, though my keeled logic never slows
sorting through the midnight revelation trove
like: I'll never be Bollywood enough
and other deadly blows

hours interpreting infill, charisma, a vinewall view
the docent moon that scales Annunciation with any luck
tomorrow ticking closer and the exuvia wake
mango slushies, dim sum zones, nine mythic attributes

in the rain tonight I can hear the worms all surfacing
through the dermal layers of unrest
gasping in the teeth of the Lebreton Street dragonesque
accumulating, I haven't slept a thing

# snakecatching

the kind of forgettable day you remember forever
that time we were snakecatching and didn't catch any
though you said for sure by Jean-Baptiste or behind the Chinese
    church
when you still wore glasses and we were determined
before I poured out all my bottled lightning
before you got perfect

I said: I told you, there are no snakes on Empress
you said: yes there is, and told me the legend of Empress Snake
and there were streetlight silhouettes like quarter notes
or bird notation or something musical swaying against the hydro
    wires
still a mystery then, the volume of my venomous heart
as I leaned listening to you against the divinity walls

# this stretch equestrian

bicycles only turn into bicycles
locked up on Bell Street
      north of Christie
      shrines to suspended velocity

it's the local metropomorphica
see that glow behind the particleboard
      they built miracles in
      this stretch equestrian

harnessed shrines and unleashed sacred
the bicycles of Bell Street change course
      see the altered cyclotaur
      half-human half-horse

# night of the mountain goats

there's nothing I can do about those regifter stars
poets ran out of thank-you notes centuries ago

and still the shine is restored in the Arthur Street sky
for speechless karmanauts to receive again tonight

may as well be a hookless shepherd of mountain goats
for all the luck I'll have herding the brilliant hanzi

grazing in the backlit heaven on every rooftop
at the intersection of Arthur and Somerset

like the trade constellations in these market windows
every conceivable gift winks inaccessible

blades and fans, porcelain beads, lanterns and false fire
good luck flags, strings of plastic stars, calm flocks of Buddha

# monkey bars

you were born with your soul in the branches
and a heart made of monkey bars
all up and down Cambridge Street
you sent kneeskin to the jubilant gods

swinging blisterpalm in the iron vines
anointed with chalk
or pennyspit breathless
blurred above the cement's primary colours

whoever you become
clambering up through your heart's scaffolding
I'll encounter you with the same wonder
as the schoolyard's wilderness of highsummer grass

# rooster machine

there's one under every city
an oily rustle in the earthwork
they found it

at Bronson and Somerset
the frost-heaving season
surfaced feathers
all through the cracks in the blacktop
an ageless heart pounding
every morning since

the hardhat archeologists arrived
steering their hatchery engines
shaped like broken birds

# dogwalker revelation

revelation, my unlikely canine dominance

we were outside the Daily Grind
I had never walked a dog before

it was almost like falling for you
easier than I thought, an anatomical pull
headed elsewhere, handed back

on Percy Street you inducted me
into the secret society of dogwalkers
you said the universe is held in the mouth of a faithful dog

you said at the end of the world
maybe there's a happy ending

if it's love, we fall

# sweet and sour pork house fate

to live laughing on Bay Street
in a house painted the colour of sweet and sour pork
that is a good fate

I lost you in a time of hungry clouds
when I couldn't tell one pillar from another
and the zodiac was nothing but empty cages

my fate was to stay in love with you until the death of poetry
in your invisibility
I wish you a better fate than my own

to live laughing on Bay Street
in a house painted the colour of sweet and sour pork
that is a good fate

if graffitichild
didn't engineer monsters

# graffitichild builds the church of sleep

janny graffitichild could tease out
even the dragons threaded in the air
and he did she with her jostling his wrist
twisted them like magician's silk
from their secret pipes in the brickwall sky
that time she dreamed he of the stained glass girl
sprawled unconscious at the intersection of nothing
her silent movie light and flickering breath
breaking a collage of bells against the heart of everywhere

and nightshifter graffitichild knew
more than anything a city needs sleep
so he whispered she to the hypnotic figurine
I'll worry you a church sweet starfish
but with grinning instinct contracted the circadian job
to the deafening reptiles she unravelled he like wires
spitting sparks from all the anxious cracks in heaven
one for every wakeful hour that graffitichild trickmaker
built the church of sleep with dragons

high in the midnight steeple he welded she those restless lizards
with engines in their mouths and poisoned nostalgia
and starving or gorged or razored with passion
the reptile mortar wrapped around and around
the darkbright girl who would dandelion vanish
if graffitichild didn't engineer monsters
to thrash a sanctuary against the freeway winds
and let sleep long for all her desperate pilgrims
curled up in the coils of her unforgiving church

# behind the lodestar

maybe if she jaywalks the horizon
and stays up before time is pieced together
hidden in the one place where there is no light
but her gemstone shoulders

dandeliongirl with her naked eye
and with heaven's marginalia
traced on the arcade of her spine
will witness the naming of the stars

before she too in her cold ecstasy
is tagged by the sextant gods
and tethered arm and mirror and arc
once more to the blade of dreams

# the last of the printer's devils

I sleep without policy and wake
in the dreamless anarchy of disbelief
oh five forty five
if I had faith in anything
it would be your terrible tetragrammaton
a prayer to the light-emitting diode
just nine minutes more / oblivion me

but in the church cold of the kitchen there you are
again digital aleph / now sigil of the coffee maker
oh five fifty seven
grovelling for your tantric concubine
if I'm going to find god it's here
a prayer to saint trafficked caffeine
nothing more urban than your rainforest stigmata

under the birdwires of another agnostic dawn
with my soma buzz and an offering of loose change
oh six or seven something
I'll wait as long as it takes / but tell me
is it tricks on or tricks off today
a prayer to the cherub committee of mass transit
clockwork miracles are all I ask

those faces behind every rush hour window
I don't believe they're dreaming of seraphim
oh look at the time
desperate heretics whispering
even to bicycle couriers as instruments of divinity
a prayer to the twelve orders and sacred operations
of souls at large in the traffic / halo us

above the text / a falling man
the last of the printer's devils
oh seven thirty nine

I log on in the age of information
and time dies
a prayer to the god of blasphemy
launch my thousand Helens of Troy

# coffee

I'm tired and know nothing of your tropic origin
whether you are smuggled by revolutionaries
out from under the half-light of prehistoric leaves
steeping in machine gun oil or shouldered down mountains
on the backs of sherpa mystics to the idling
convoy of hipsters arrived on their fair trade vespas
or whether you are handpicked by mermaids exploited
on the banks of equatorial seas I'm so tired

tired and my imagination keeps me ignorant
as I anoint you with a first world mythology
from now on you are the nymphomaniac's midwife
in a dreamless downtown at the beginning of time
stories about a threshold city that cannot wake
until a volley of black pigeons signals your birth
as though from every tower window every mother
leans to crack her sheets against the unresisting sky

# signs and wonders

calculating how old I was each time
I believed I became the person I was supposed to become
ten seventeen twenty-seven twenty-eight thirty-five thirty-eight
watching the songtrees nod crow silhouettes
against a sky all the colours of a failed marriage
number seven bus stop five-thirty eighteen may twenty-ten

commuting in the precaffeinated civil dawn
I get closer to dreaming the more conscious I become
aware of an angry whisper of snakeskin
trailing from the four-forty-five alarm all the way down
        Beechwood
where neighbours board and murmur like eyelids
what I interpret as friendly reports of signs and wonders

remembering we were in a library a grocery store a parking lot
        a theatre
or somewhere worried the numbers were wrong
too many or too few kids husbands wives lovers allies
struggling to confront the great terribleness of meaning
only to recognize the outstretched scales of the dream for what
        they are
not the dust of consciousness transformed but merely dust

reading the spine of your paperback reflected in the window
whoever you are in your transparent beauty I never see your face
but my skin and yours with a mighty hand and with an
        outstretched arm
and suddenly twenty-three october and still this cricket in my
        blood
like a choir of clotheslines like harp strings from house to house
and I too have been who I am more than once coming and going

# the martyr of hubcaps

I saw the martyr of hubcaps
dancing with his depression-era dog
the divinity jigging like a pirate
while the eyepatch mutt
leaped question marks
around his knees

# half-skinned rabbit

you know I walk too fast so yesterday I recognized the animal but
        not the violence
I thought maybe it was a magician's prop half-sprung from an
        infinite top hat
but now I know for sure the device is leaping out of itself

get here somehow and I'll take you to see the half-skinned rabbit
this civil city is only one knife away from living on its tanner
        outskirts
eccentric and fearless and prolific like a memory conjured by scent

some days the sun cuts a hole in the storefronts and opens the
        beating meat of things
all soaked in acid and urine and tight as a harness and old as
        sandals and coded as a book
and I laugh and thank the muses for law leather and stretch my
        hand into whatever new glove this is

get here somehow and we'll read in circles about the bush knife
        and the shive of bread
I thought it was a passage from wonderland but couldn't decipher
        the sacrificial march hare
or the compass of flame or the alchemical language of the tin cup
        and the parcel of spoons and the frozen hair

the end of the coil said camper's diary and I saw this was the hard
        joy of an older ritual
twenty-five december eighteen-twenty-six still sleeping with every
        foot to the fire
still at the centre of this city circa may two-thousand-nine in the
        dizzy sun

on the half-skinned rabbit in the gloved hands in the fire in the
         anonymous throats of the merry campers
in our city in our bodies in the hole in the pedestrians in the art of
         my happiness carved in the sidewalk
so get here somehow and we'll relive the half I just invented and
         the half you can't recall

# the wind as a teenager with chrome

an empty parking lot proves anything is possible
wonder at the twenty-four hour metro
locked up for the long weekend
all its serrated expanse of concrete past date as of yesterday
distilled to sacred space

and written in chain link
the history of something that tried to force its way in
something that tried to bend its way out
the supernatural darkness of a hushed supermarket
luminous chrome

in the time of year of running down hills
when your tongue is on the roof of the sky
of course you're skating here
teenage wind
I wish I could wait for nothing the way you do

# Ferris Wheel

tell me the Ferris Wheel is coming
I'm on the long walkhome and need to know the Ferris Wheel
      is coming

tell me a flatbed convoy is clouding through a godfearing flatland
coming hard with the Ferris Wheel

the laststretch somewhere
the marathon cargo and floodlight resolve

tell me something is being assembled in the wrenching dark
tell me it's coming

as though it's love this time
this time finally it's a front-of-the-line cliffedge arrival

where all we need is a deep breath and our no-going-back-now
      hearts
if the Ferris Wheel is coming


every day this city makes room for the cantilever miracle
in every dragonfly weedlot and demolition arcade

until there's nothing we can keep of the old places
except throwstones and chainlink cut through to the vacancy
      elsewhere

as though nothing is coming
not even the permission to miss you this way

and the graffiti and bloodletting grass
unbroken and unmoved, down the avenue's endless lines

unless the Ferris Wheel is coming
and that's why the gasstation is gone, the brickhome, the stand of
      trees

to make up for every time I disappointed you
gone for the Ferris Wheel to come


tell me
tonight the city is swollen with fireworks

and from the bridge life is permanent skyline
where we can dream the silhouette aloft on the dark

and the rustthroat cello of restless secrets, shifting against the
      sundown wind
and the strings of whitelight and faith for a quarter and regrets
      bargained away

and the mirror of strangers and all the moving parts of love
so tell me the Ferris Wheel is coming

the way you told me the seedstar and the road and the hush of
      longing
and we stood innocent in the gravel until the bar came down

and we were up there in the calliope light, in the carnival arc
in the Ferris Wheel

# in spite of the road crew, joy

the house is shaking
>like love

unhappy engines
>are loud

looking for secret roads
>lower and lower

the discarded street
>is sifted

lifting like sleep
>through windows

grey misted
>while thinking goes

one moth at a time
>to blink

at the bright brown
>digging sound

# inanna jammer

queen of wheels
>     no city without you
>     all of us in the suicide seats
>     circulate your name

>     inanna jammer

the atomic clock will never catch you
>     all your lovers are statues
>     we grew up falling down on you
>     without shame

>     inanna chaotica

travelling goddesspeed
>     on your routes and arteries
>     for you we hang these prayershoes
>     on every hydro line

>     inanna creatrix

skin tight halo
>     our friday incarnate
>     the revolution goes horizontal
>     all the arts that pierce your flesh

>     inanna ovational

crossbone butterfly
>     we circulate your name
>     the revolution goes vertical
>     all the arts that pierce the clouds

>     inanna jammer

# terminal city rollergirls
### for Mel

last stop before the ocean falls into the coast
because even cities run out of breath after an uncertain distance
out in the Kerrisdale trophy train tracks and consignment stores

where the continent drops me off at the arena
me and a demographic armoured in stars
under the laced up white leather light

the fast cage lamps and the durable plastic moon
forget days ago it was snowing on Caprica
tonight it's full summer in the playground of the gods

I'll know for sure at the roller derby

the way paint knows all the way down Hastings
wood can't be trusted
look at how the colours are escaping everywhere

above the cherry neon concrete
in the ancestral prism of the rafters
the bleacher shadows are switched on like magnolia blossoms

the beauty of blurred faces
every fugitive song
buries another needle in my transistor heart

know me when you see me at the roller derby

I'm the one getting blisters just by looking around
eye contact is my only strategy
all hands and blind faith like a whip

hips are lower in Vancouver
there are no sheet metal warning signs for that
just ransom note graphics

because life is a technique with ball bearings
a genealogy of pseudonyms
and tshirts come to the rescue of civilization one at a time

we'll know for sure at the roller derby

I dream everything beyond the zamboni doors is skatable territory
a flat track universe
where we're all jammers in the clear

a mirrorball constellation of urban legends
muse of crushes and our lady of last chance
queen of sister cities

breathless mother of the revolution
and the goddess of crowd noise
after this place everywhere else is just echolocation

know me when you see me at the roller derby

even if cliffs in Kerrisdale hide behind the Eden epic trees
moss won't take the shape of anything standing still
because nothing will stand still at the arena

we're all runaway totem poles
one face on top of the other
the only thing we take with us is our secret identity

and we'll all be home in four hours
flying toward night like we grew up to be superheroes
this is as close as we get

I'll know for sure at the roller derby

# parkingchrist

said a prayer to the trinity
to nail this three-point turn

said a prayer to the parkingchrist
to find space at his table

no circling purgatory
no temporal signs

no meters or thou shalt nots
no bylaw judases

just you and I parallel
so a prayer to the trinity

to find space at your table
said a prayer to the parkingchrist

# loudspeaker

loudspeaker
your rush hour vestments

loudspeaker
who governs the decibels

loudspeaker
your crisis of angels

loudspeaker
who chases his own voice

loudspeaker
your sunday vigilantes

loudspeaker
who scales the fire escape

loudspeaker
your labyrinth of echoes

loudspeaker
who rappels in the masonry

loudspeaker
your siren majestic

loudspeaker
who makes the jump

loudspeaker
your congregation of roadies

loudspeaker
who detonates attention

          loudspeaker
your distorted identity

          loudspeaker
              who pilots the feedback

          loudspeaker
your icons unlimited

          loudspeaker
              who triggers the megaphone

          loudspeaker
everlasting

          loudspeaker

# saint corporate citizen

pray for us saint corporate citizen
your miraculous birth from a falling tube of fluorescent light
your shower of glass and mercury
class action icons in our eyes and lungs
give hope to the shattered

defend us from the demons of blowback
and all their subcontractors
gutter rain and innuendo and the shrapnel of ambition
anything that might blow up in our face
timelines, typos, marriage

patron of overtime
you ascend beyond the seraphim of rush hour
promoted so many times you're invisible
sustain us with your open door policy
while we pray one day to find the door

# Chemistry City

I dreamed of your metro shoulders
leaning in the vespa crush of Chemistry City
your rabbit tshirt and rocket dogs and my sense of direction
and a camera we share without taking pictures
just so our fingers will touch
if our eyes wander

where our lifesize conversations cast their own shadows
endless meridians across a plaza of birds and tourists and busker
       rings
and I ask why they're seagulls if there's no sea
and you say they're plazagulls
and I think instead somewhere a birdless sea has lost its identity
and you say anyway they're pigeons

and that's how you rescue things
you could save even an ocean from drowning
and that's why I'm suddenly in the arms of architecture
with a balaclava and a list of your lovers
scaling fire escapes to ransack every apartment in their memory
to thieve your heart and your heat from their experience

I know it's a waste of time
like a sundial in a paparazzi swarm
when I wake at home I don't quite wake at home
all the lines in this city still take their shape from your body
the angle from your thigh in my hand to your heel sunk in the
       mattress
the naked skyline waiting patiently for night to come

# the Tower of Babel

O blessed infidelity
O candles collapsed into swans
O all the fireproof birds of heaven and
    this illusion we are building something
        just because our shadows get longer

        without resisting the book I held open on your back
            that time in our skin
        you were face down under
         the history of architecture
      having me reading in you altered
      the jumping lines and breathless
    O the golden flesh of the gods and
   O the arena of bulls and
  O the making of bricks in the sun and
 O the scribes bent to their work and
how my hands on the open pages of your back and
a fist of sheets and
under the confusion of tongues
how we designed
in joy out loud
the Tower of Babel

      you heard

in this position of strength I confess I am in a perpetual state of seduction
      everyone and everything is doing it to me and I
        I need to stay up late in you
      to survey the demolition of language and
   from me this string of curses each one a promise
  to learn you again and again even if I
I must strike the sky with arrows and

I heard

now I would cast my inconstant shadow on seventy-two scholars
if it's the only way to get this thing built I will
I will crouch like an abecedarian and
fake ignorance in my infinite knowledge
    for any man come with angry eyes and the dust of the work
        on his shoulders and the white rain and the rockingchair and
            a shoreline serrated by seraphim wings and


    we heard

        now ruin this thing before god gets here and
    with his heavy mouth and his tool like the beak of an ibis
            he has his way with us both
        you'll be his blindfolded disoriented stairfaller and
            I'll be his deactivated activist and
        O his apocryphal white van and
        O his sacred warehouse of indoctrination and
    O his excited sodium light and
O our tower like a forgetmenaut rocket

rocketeered into the white collar asphalt downtown
            where it's just skulls that make us beautiful and

when you go full amnesia on me
        I swear I won't remember anything you said and

when the nightshift industry in me is all lies anyway
        you swear you'll still pilot brick after brick and

    that's how the king of the damned and the queen of labyrinths
            lying
        built the Tower of Babel

# the system of worship at intersections

keep your medieval jackrabbits
and the whole system of worship
at intersections / you tourist

the somewhere distance you've travelled
is all the remembrance I need
of you and the pope of postcards

a mass of pigeons / you tourist
I saw my heart escape today
in the shape of a flock of birds

you can abandon me but not
the trinity of the crossroad
sovereign courtesan troubadour

eventually even you
tourist / will hit the somewhere lights

# umbrella hag

no shelter, love
she'll never have one
and neither will you
they're too much like lovers
folding backward before the least wind
so empty underneath
though the weather never comes from one direction
they're sadder than the rain
so she'll break every one, love
no one misses umbrellas
when they're gone

# behind every furnace a paraffin boy

blameless and terrible the paraffin boy
the paraffin boy who fell in love with fire

the ticking of his knitting needle fingers
at night trying to hold in his spilling heart

the candle wax heart of the paraffin boy
son of an asphyxiated pilot light

and the rabbit priest of carnivore angels
consumed in the ruby teeth of devotion

behind every furnace a paraffin boy
the paraffin boy who fell in love with fire

# a prayer to the angel of death

if we must fall together
riding a desperate arc like cursed lovers
if at last your hands find the bones stretching my flesh
and lift bruises across me
like breath blown on a mirror

don't let your silver shoulders cut my hands
don't spill this city on me
this architecture of black feathers
don't let me hide and heave against you
like an angry moon
don't let the simian night
shatter the window and dance my dreams into rags
don't let me slide from your limbs
your soft wrists pressed against the constellations
as I fall through the lonely atmosphere
clutching the jagged stars

# dollhousehead

and when the building's almost dead
there shall dwell a dollhousehead

> her broken mouth and rabbit heart
> her splintered mudras in the dark

and when the garden's overgrown
a dollhousehead abides alone

> sorting through with insect grace
> the silted contents of her face

and when the slum's in state ignored
a dollhousehead on every floor

> and crouching on each balcony
> a dollhousehead on virgin knee

and when the cities all are bled
at last the reign of dollhousehead

# the apocalypse of graffitichild

here is the vandalism that will never fade
fathomed artless graffitichild even as the paint was crying still
that prolific time she decked he every other soul
with the art of being lonely in crowds
and hysterical that graffitichild forlorn dissolved his vision her
and the holy noiseboys and dirtgirls with their braids of electricity
and the spirits of flicked cigarettes and the blessed jester refuse
and all the jammers imps saints and neon godthings
to the very skyline of the metropantheon suspended

their citywide dominion for the last gridlocked transmission
as the angel of antennas with her ear to graffitichild's lips
amplified the bad news: graffitichild she said he alone I saw
the one rabbit fall from the one dog's mouth and that is the fall
        of love
the oracle in alleys of distraction vanish and that is the fall of love
free hotel on fire and the nevermore man blameless and that is the
        fall of love
no muses and no addicts at dawn and that is the fall of love
at last the death of dragons and the rush of dandelion seeds and
        that is the fall of love
and every city fallen dollhouse small and that is the fall of love

but it can only get so cold he smiled she graffitichild
before love arrives with every muscle to build another city
and in that city the chosen few will learn to dance
and in our numbers the chosen few will be infinite
janitor stripper bureaucrat librarian transitcop
king busker poet madman jaywalker journeyman neighbour
everyone alive in the congested demographic of the urbanation
        entire
clapping the intro of everything like it's the summer of cities
        at last and
onetwo one onetwo one onetwo one onetwo

## about the author

Steven Artelle lives in Ottawa, where he works at Library and Archives Canada. He has a Ph.D. in English Literature from the University of Western Ontario. In 2013 AngelHousePress published his chapbook *four hundred rabbits*, an excerpt from a work in progress. *Metropantheon* is his first collection of poetry.